i Rode My Bike Without A Grown Up

By: Patrice Thomas

To order additional copies of this book, contact:
Xlibris
1-888-795-4274
www.Xlibris.com
Orders@Xlibris.com

ISBN: Softcover   978-1-4628-2943-9
        EBook   978-1-4691-2884-9

Print information available on the last page

Rev. date: 12/02/2019

Hi, I'm Dorian and today we're gonna read about a boy who learns how to ride his bike, without any grown ups.

Yes, all by himself. His father coached, but Dorian did it, all on his own.

So sit back while Dorian tell his story, and maybe, just maybe one day you can do it too.

Chapter 1

It's almost Christmas and I'm so happy. Mg little brother Donavan and I are hoping to get new bicycles this year.

We already have bikes, but they have training wheels on them. This year hopefully we can get the big bogs bikes.

Chapter 2

Today is Christmas Eve. Everyone is so happy including myself. Mommy and daddy are wrapping gifts and singing Christmas carols. I hope Santa got our letter, because we really want those bicycles.

Chapter 3

Our parents always say get to bed early, because Santa is coming. So we prepared him some cookies and milk. Before bed we pray and ask God to watch over us, our family and everybody in the world.

Chapter 4

Today is Christmas and like every year, we wake up to the sound of Christmas music. Mommy and daddy are ready for us to charge in the living room and open our gifts.

Chapter 5

I told my brother these gifts are great, but where did Santa leave our big boy bicycles. Daddy looked at us and said, boys we have one last gift in the back.

Rushing to the back and to our surprise, we saw two of the most beautiful big boy bicycles. We each had our own.

Chapter 6

Now that we have them, we must learn to ride them. We asked our daddy for help and he replied, I can teach you, but you have to learn how to ride yourself.

So we listened to all his instructions.

Chapter 7

Week after week we tried, but we could not get the hang of it. By this time daddy sat us down and said, first you must learn how to balance yourself and peddle.

It worked, but we still fell down. He pushed us off, but we could not make it around the house without falling off.

Chapter 8

Daddy finally said, maybe you should try to ride by yourself.

So we did. At first I was scared, but did pretty good. As the days past we got better and better at it with all the practice.

Chapter 9

Our sisters Mercedes & Tasha joined in to give us advise. They would say
when you get started don't stop, Keep peddling.

So on the next day we got on our bikes and started peddling and Kept at it. We began to get better and stronger.

Chapter 10

One day mommy and daddy went to Thomas Ville and Donovan and myself staged home with Mercedes and Alexis. Alexis and Mercedes are best friends.

Donovan and I were outside with them. We were practicing riding our bikes and I must say doing really good. Before I knew what was happening I was riding around the house without falling all by myself, with no help from any grown up.

We told Mercedes, but she didn't notice. So I kept on riding, with Donovan behind me.

Chapter 11

When mommy and daddy returned home we were so happy to show them how I learned to ride my big bog bike.

Donavan running getting mommy and daddy. Dorian knows how to ride his bike. Our parents were like show us, so I did. Donavan said, watch this, go Dorian show mommy and daddy you can do it.

At first he took off slow, but he didn't fall and before we knew it he was coming around the house. We were like Dorian you did it. He was like I told you daddy. All I could say was you sure did son and I am so proud of you.

Chapter 12

After that I was riding every where. I even helped my little brother Donavan learn to ride his bike, (along with daddy).

We all helped, but it was Dorian who never gave up. He really did learn how to ride his big boy bike all by himself.

Maybe one day you too can learn to ride your bike by yourself. GOOD luck.

THE END

Printed in the United States
By Bookmasters